Greenhaven World History Program

GENERAL EDITORS

Malcolm Yapp
Margaret Killingray
Edmund O'Connor

Cover design by Gary Rees

ISBN 0-89908-017-0 Paper Edition
ISBN 0-89908-042-1 Library Edition

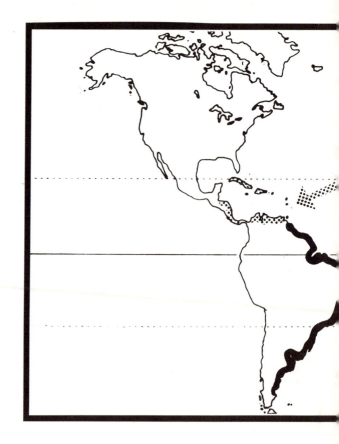

First published in Great Britain 1975 by
GEORGE G. HARRAP & CO. LTD.
© George C. Harrap & Co. Ltd. 1975

COLUMBUS

by Desmond Painter

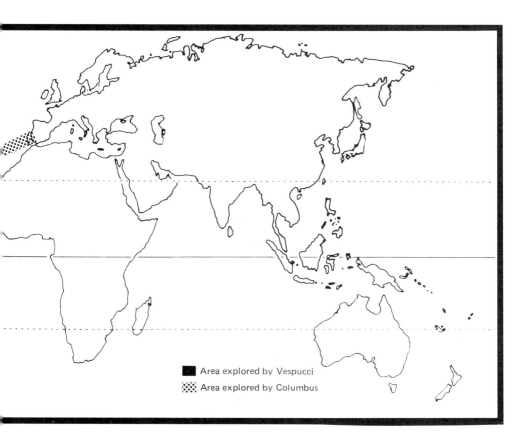

Area explored by Vespucci
Area explored by Columbus

Greenhaven Press, Inc.
577 SHOREVIEW PARK ROAD
ST. PAUL, MN 55112

This portrait of Columbus by an unknown painter hangs in his native city of Genoa

Not very much is known about the early life of Christopher Columbus. He was born in 1451 in the Italian sea port of Genoa. His father was a wool merchant, and Christopher helped in the family business. He probably did not go to school much, but he did go on several short voyages for his father.

GENOA

Genoa was one of the great Italian trading cities. Ships went from her port to other cities all over the Mediterranean and beyond: some went as far as the Black Sea in the east, and Flanders and England in the north. In those days Europe was not as we know it today. France and England were powerful and important, but most of Europe was divided up into small states, often consisting of no more than a single town. Each state was like a little country on its own, with its own laws, and ruled by its own king or prince. The Italian city-states were among the richest and most prosperous in Europe. (*Leonardo da Vinci*)* And yet, compared with the great industrial towns of today, these cities of the fifteenth century were tiny. Life was harder then, and nature could be a powerful enemy. When the Genoese sailors set out in their tiny ships (even the biggest of them was unlikely to be larger than 400 or 500 tonnes), they knew that a storm could destroy them in a matter of minutes.

COLUMBUS IN PORTUGAL

It was on a voyage from Genoa in 1476, when Columbus was twenty-five years old, that he met just such a storm, and was shipwrecked on the coast of Portugal. His brother, Bartholomew Columbus, was already in Portugal, working as a chart maker in Lisbon, and Christopher decided to join him there. During the next few years he caught up on his education and learnt to read and write. He also learnt a lot more about sailing and the sea, went on voyages in the Atlantic, and married the daughter of the Commander of Porto Santo, a Portuguese island near Madeira. Columbus studied the Commander's charts and log books, and many books on geography. By the time he was thirty he was an experienced sailor who knew many important people in Portugal, and he had worked out a plan to make himself rich and famous.

THE INDIES, CATHAY AND CIPANGO

Columbus's plan was to sail to the Indies, Cathay and Cipango. Cathay and Cipango were the names given at that time to China and Japan. 'The Indies' was a vague name which covered an area including India itself and the islands now known as the East Indies: much as we might say 'the lands of the East'. Few Europeans had been to these places, but they thought they were lands of fabulous wealth. One of the main reasons for this was a book written by Marco Polo, two hundred years before Columbus's time; but it was almost the only first-hand information there was. Columbus had his own copy of the book, and wrote notes in the margin of it. In his book, Marco Polo wrote about the great riches and magnificence of China, which he had seen (D1)** (*Traditional China*), and the abundance of gold in Japan, which he had only heard about. (D2)

THE SPICE TRADE

Gold, jewels and fine silk were all things which Columbus hoped to bring home from his planned voyage. He also hoped to bring spices: cloves, pepper, nutmeg and several others. In the fifteenth century these were great luxuries, and rich people in Europe paid very high prices for them; especially for cloves, which grew

---

*Titles in brackets refer to other booklets in the Program

**The reference (D) indicates the numbered documents at the end of this book

tiſſimū bȝ qui nulli tributariʼ é Idoíés inſule ydolatre ſūt
et oés nude. ābulant mares et femine ⸗ quilibȝ vereçūda
opit páno vno Idullū bladū bn̄t excepto riſo Carnibʼ ri
ſo et lacte viuūt babūdanciá bn̄t ſeminū ſolūmó de quibʼ
oleū faciūt bn̄t biricios melioꝛes mūdi qui ibi creſcūt Ali
nū eciā bn̄t de arboꝛibʼ de quibʼ dcīn̄ ſup in regno ſama⸗
rá In bac iſula lapides pcioſi inueniūt qui dicūt Rubini
qui i regionibʼ alijs nó inueniūt vel bn̄t. Multi eni eciā
ſapbiri et topacij et amatiſte ibi ſunt multiȝ alij lapides p
cioſi Rex buius inſule babet pulcbrioꝛe rubinū qui vnꝙ
fuit viſus in boc mūdo babet enim vniʼ palme longitudi⸗
né et ad menſurá groſſicici braebij bois Eſt āt ſplendidʼ
ſup modū onmi macula carens adeo vt ignis ardens vide
atur eſſe Magnʼ kaam Cublay nuncios ſuos direxit ad
illū rogans vt pfatū lapide illi donaret et ipe donaret ei
valoꝛé vnius ciuitatis D. ul rn̄dit ꝙ lapis ille ſuoꝛ erat an
ceſſoꝛū nulli eū vnꝙ homini daret Iduiʼ inſule boíes bel
licoſi non ſunt ſed valde viles D. uando autē bella cū aliq
bus babent de alienis ꝑtibus ſtipendiarios vocant et ſpe
cialiter ſarracenos

De regno maabar   Capitulū xxiij.
Ltra inſulá ſeylā ad miliaria xl inueniūt maabar ꝙ ma⸗
ioꝛ india nūcupaꝛ Idó āut é inſula ⸗ terra firma. In
bac puincia quiȝ reges ſūt Pꝛouicia é nobiliſſiā et diuſſ
ſima ſup modū In pmo buiʼ puicie rex é noíe Seudeba
i quo regno ſūt margarite i copia maxiá In mari eni buiʼ
puicie é maris braebiū ſeu ſinus inꝶ firmā terrā et inſulā
ꝙ vbi nó eſt aquaꝝ pfūditas vltra decem vel duodeci
paſſus et alicubi vltra duos Ibi inueniūt margarite ſup
océ Mercatoꝛes eni diuerſi ſocietates ad inuicē faciūt ⁊
bn̄t naues magnas et puas boíesȝ códucūt qui deſcen
dūt ad pfūdū aquarū et capiūt cócbilia in quibus ſunt

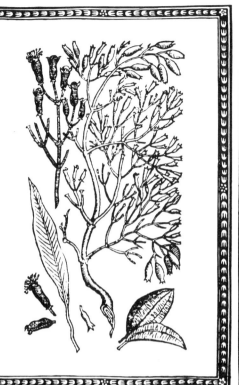

Old engraving showing cloves (left) and nutmegs (right), two of the spices Columbus hoped to bring back from the East

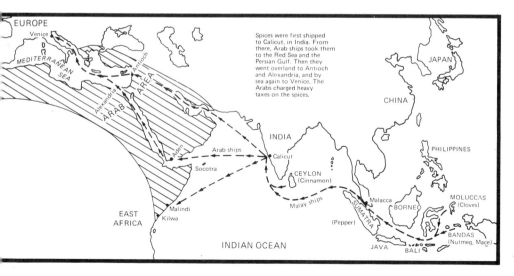

Spices were first shipped to Calicut, in India. From there, Arab ships took them to the Red Sea and the Persian Gulf. Then they went overland to Antioch and Alexandria, and by sea again to Venice. The Arabs charged heavy taxes on the spices.

This map shows how the Arabs controlled the spice trade between the East Indies and Europe

what a fortune Columbus would make!

PRESTER JOHN

But gold and spices were not the only reasons why Columbus wanted to sail to the Indies. Christian Europe had for centuries been threatened by warlike, non-Christian peoples from the east. First the Arabs, who had conquered the Middle East and North Africa, and thrust through Spain into France itself (*Muhammad and the Arab Empire*): then came the Mongols whose empire reached from China across Asia, and into Russia and Eastern Europe. (*Chingis Khan and the Mongol Empire*) Now it was the Ottoman Turks, who already controlled the Christian holy places in Palestine, and were attacking at sea, and up the Danube towards Belgrade and Vienna. (*Suleyman and the Ottoman Empire*) One of the great hopes of the leaders of Europe was to find a Christian ally in Asia or Africa who could help to hold back the Muslim enemy and regain the Holy Land. Columbus hoped that he might help here, too, for Marco Polo had also written about the legendary Prester (Priest) John, a Christian prince. Some said that he lived in Africa and ruled a great kingdom; others, that his realm was in Asia. Marco Polo wrote that his kingdom was on the borders of China: but he had not actually been there. Perhaps Columbus could find him: if not, at least he could bring the Christian religion to the idol-worshippers of the Indies.

WEST TO THE INDIES

So far, Columbus's dream of sailing to the Indies was not new. Others hoped to do the same, and for the same reasons. What was new about Columbus's plan was that he was going to reach the Indies by sailing *west*. Everyone knew the world was round, and Marco Polo had written rather vaguely of a strait leading into the Indian Ocean from the east. (D3) This strait, known by Columbus's time as the strait of Cattigara, was shown on maps such as the one drawn by Henricus Martellus. Other maps, such as Toscanelli's showed islands in the Atlantic where Columbus could stop on his way to China, Japan and Cattigara. Portuguese ships by this time were already exploring far down the coast of Africa. In 1488, Bartholomew Dias rounded the Cape of Good Hope and showed the way open to the Indies by the eastward route. (*Spices and Civilizations*) Columbus thought his westward route would be quicker and easier. We now know that his maps were wrong in some important ways; and he also made two crucial mistakes in his calculations. He thought that the world was much smaller than it is, and that Asia was much bigger than it is.

HOW BIG IS A DEGREE?

The circumference of the earth is divided into 360 degrees: but how long is a degree? Ancient and modern geographers disagreed. Ptolemy was the most respected

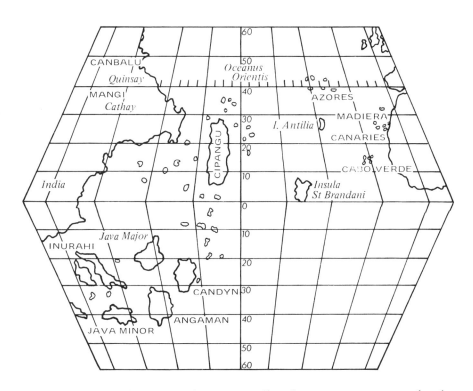

CANBALU
Quinsay
MANGI
Cathay
India
Java Major
INURAHI
JAVA MINOR

60
50 Oceanus Orientis
40
30
20
10
0
10
20
30
40
50
60

CIPANGU

AZORES
MADIERA
I. Antilia
CANARIES
CABO VERDE
Insula St Brandani

CANDYN
ANGAMAN

This map was made in 1474 by Toscanelli, who sent a copy to Columbus. It shows a short ocean crossing westwards from Africa to Japan

authority, but Columbus chose to follow the Arab geographer Alfragan. Unfortunately, Columbus did not read Alfragan's book correctly, and finished up by thinking that a degree was only 83 kilometres long at the Equator. (D4) He also tried to find the position of Japan by taking an estimate from another ancient geography book and adding 'corrections' based on Marco Polo's guesses. By this method Columbus calculated that the distance from Portugal *eastwards* to Japan covered about 280 degrees. If he went *westwards* he could stop first at the Canary Islands, about nine degrees west. From the Canaries there would be less than seventy degrees to travel. At 83 kilo-

metres to a degree that meant only about 5,800 kilometres, and Toscanelli's map showed islands which he could stop at on the way. In fact, the distance to Japan was about four times as great as Columbus believed. If he had known the truth he would never have set out!

THE QUEEN OF SPAIN BACKS COLUMBUS

Columbus had difficulty in getting anyone to back his plan. He tried Portugal, Spain, France and England. Eventually, almost by chance, the Queen of Spain was persuaded by a courtier to agree to the plan, and an elaborate document was drawn up.

An old engraving showing Columbus' ship, the Santa Maria

Columbus was given the title of Admiral, and appointed governor of any new lands which he might discover. He could take 10 per cent of the value of all the gold, jewels, spices or other merchandise that was brought back to Spain, and he had the right to a one-eighth share in any future voyage. (D5)

SPAIN

Although we talk now about Spain as a country like France or England, in Columbus's time it had only just been united by the marriage of Ferdinand and Isabela, the rulers of Aragon and Castile. This is why some of the documents in this book refer to 'Castila' rather than 'Spain'. Even so, important parts of Spain (especially Catalonia) were still not fully under the control of the King.

But Spain had even bigger problems abroad. The king of Spain had many important possessions in other parts of Europe – in Italy, Burgundy (now in south-eastern France) and the Netherlands (modern Holland and Belgium). These possessions were sometimes (especially in the case of the Spanish Netherlands) a source of wealth; but they were more often a source of worry and expense. The people who lived in these areas were liable to revolt, while other European rulers (especially the King of France) were liable to try to take them by force. On top of all this the kings of Spain saw themselves as leaders in the defence of the Catholic Church, first against the Turks, then against the Protestants, who later caused whole areas of Christian Europe to break away from the Church. (*Luther, Erasmus and Loyola*) All these commitments resulted in continuous and enormous expense, and the rulers of Spain welcomed any possibility of increasing their wealth.

THE FIRST VOYAGE

On 3rd August 1492 Columbus

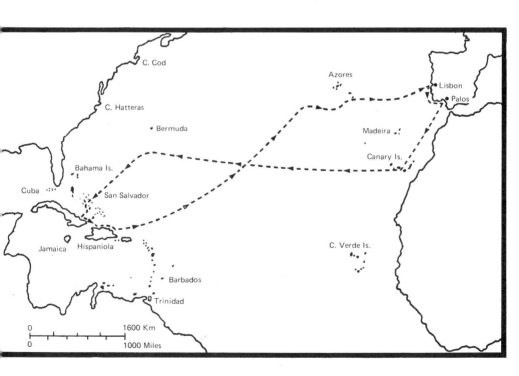

This map shows the route Columbus followed on his first and most famous voyage across the Atlantic

set sail from Palos in Southern Spain with three ships: two caravels, the *Niña* and the *Pinta* and the flagship *Santa Maria*. These ships were tiny by modern standards. The *Santa Maria* was the biggest at 100 tonnes: a modern ocean liner is two or three hundred times as big! The whole expedition totalled ninety men, most of them local seamen from the Palos area. They set out carrying a letter from the King and Queen of Spain to the Grand Khan, whom Marco Polo had said was the ruler of China. On 6th September they left the Canary Islands and headed west into the unknown. For ocean

sailing the caravels were converted from lateen rig to square rig.

Lateen rig meant that one or more of the sails was hung fore and aft, along the line of the ship. This idea had come from the Arabs. With a lateen rig, a ship could sail into the wind and manoeuvre easily in shallow coastal waters. With a square rig, the sails were hung across the line of the ship, which could go faster, but needed a wind from behind. Even square rigged, Columbus's ships could only cover about 160 kilometres a day at best, and after thirty days out of sight of land his crew were getting worried. They threatened to mutiny and turn

This rather fanciful engraving, made some time afterwards, shows Columbus arriving in the New World. He is being greeted by Indians with gifts

This engraving of a scene in Cuba shows what the island would have looked like to Columbus

back. But, after thirty-three days at sea, land was sighted on 12th October at about two o'clock in the morning: Watling Island in the Bahamas. Columbus was delighted: he explored some of the islands, believing that they were near the mainland of Asia. He sent an enthusiastic report back to Spain (D6) and reached home again as a hero.

THE POPE DIVIDES THE WORLD

The King and Queen of Spain hastened to stake their claim to the rich trade of the Indies, which they believed was now going to bring them enormous wealth. The Portuguese had discovered the way round the southern tip of Africa, and would soon be in India by the eastward route. The Spaniards wanted to make sure that nobody was going to compete with them on their western route, so they went to the only accepted international authority there was: the Pope. An agreement was reached to mark a line on the map to divide the lands of Portugal from those of Spain, and a treaty was signed with great ceremony on 2nd July 1494 at the little town of Tordesillas. (D7) As it turned out there were more quarrels to come, because nobody knew exactly where the line was, or whether it applied in the Pacific Ocean as well as the Atlantic: and of course explorers of other countries did

Building La Navidad, Columbus' first colony in Hispaniola

not see why Spain and Portugal should divide the world between them anyway. Nobody asked the people living in the new lands that were going to be taken over.

COLUMBUS'S SECOND VOYAGE

There was no lack of support for Columbus's second voyage in September 1493. Everyone wanted to get a share of the promised wealth. This time Columbus was not going to explore, but to exploit his previous discovery. He hoped to make contact with the Grand Khan and establish trade with China and

Japan; but he also hoped to set up a Spanish colony in the Indies, and convert the natives to Christianity. A fleet of seventeen ships carried stores for six months – plants and seeds, animals, and six priests.

Columbus was a bad geographer, but a good sailor, and usually got where he wanted to go. He headed for Martinique, the nearest island in the West Indies, which he had heard about on his first voyage. His course was very accurate, but he was carried a little way north by currents which he did not know about, and arrived at Dominica. He made his way back to Hispaniola, where he had left a small garrison the previous year.

Now his troubles began. The garrison had all been murdered.

Columbus established a new colony, but things did not go well. The climate was unhealthy, the spices did not seem to be there, though Columbus kept sending plants hopefully back to Spain. There was gold, but not much, and it was not easy to get. The Spanish settlers became more and more discontented and complained about Columbus. He had promised them wealth, but all they got were short rations, hardship and disease. Columbus could not cope: he was a sailor, not a governor. By the spring of 1496 things had got so bad that a commissioner from Spain came to investigate. Columbus decided to return to try and retrieve his reputation.

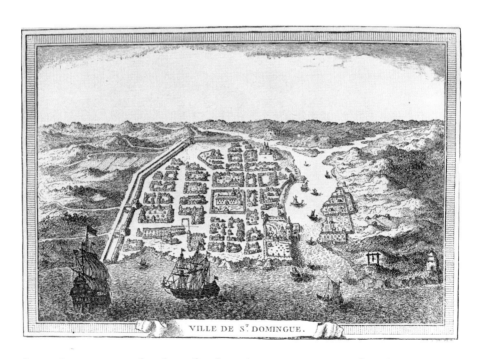

VILLE DE S.^T DOMINGUE.

Santa Domingo, Columbus' final settlement in Hispaniola. This engraving was probably made about a hundred years after Columbus, and shows a well-laid out Spanish-style town

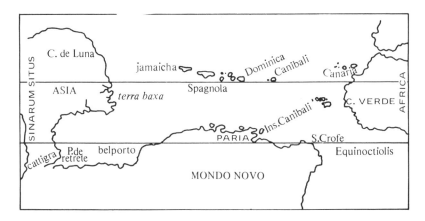

This map, made by Columbus' brother Bartholomew in 1503 shows that although Columbus thought South America was a new continent, (Mondo Novo), he thought Cuba was part of Asia

The house in Valladolid where Columbus spent his last years

THE LATER VOYAGES

The second voyage, which had started so well, had ended in miserable failure. Columbus was discredited and disgraced, and although he made two more voyages, and visited the mainland of South and Central America, his reputation never recovered. He complained bitterly to the King and Queen (D8) and still insisted to the end of his days that he had found a way to Asia: if only people would believe him and back him, he would yet find a way to the Grand Khan and the wealth of Cathay and the Indies. (D9) His brother Bartholomew loyally supported him, and showed his discoveries as part of Asia on a map drawn in 1503, but meanwhile other discoveries and calculations were being made which finally proved Columbus wrong.

AMERIGO VESPUCCI

Vespucci is one of the most important people who proved Columbus wrong. He was a very skilled geographer and important explorer, who actually discovered more unknown land than any other European of that time. He was born in 1454, the son of a businessman in Florence, a rich and flourishing city in northern Italy. Like Columbus, he studied the ancient geographers and read Marco Polo. Like Columbus, he wanted to discover the Strait of Cattigara by sailing westwards to the Indies. Like Columbus, he had good experience of ships and the sea. But, unlike Columbus, he got his sums right, and proved it on two voyages.

VESPUCCI'S FIRST VOYAGE

By 1499 Columbus had made three of his four voyages. Vespucci was sure that many of Columbus's claims were fantastic, and he managed to get himself appointed as geographer to a Spanish expedition sailing to the Indies under the command of Ojeda. Vespucci's ship separated from Ojeda's, and Vespucci reached the coast of Brazil on 27th June 1499. He was the first European to see it. During the next three months he explored 5,000 kilometres of coastline between the easternmost point of Brazil at Cape São Roque, and Venezuela. He went 160 kilometres up the estuary of the Amazon river and found it twenty-six kilometres wide even there. But, more important, Vespucci used the voyage to make observations and calculations.

THE PROBLEM OF LONGITUDE

It was possible in Vespucci's time to calculate *latitude* quite accurately. A sailor could tell how far north or south he was by measuring the angle between the horizon and a star, or the sun, and then looking up his position in a book. There were various instruments for doing this, of which the most popular were the astrolabe

This portrait of Vespucci was painted some years after his death

and the cross staff. On the other hand, it was extremely difficult to calculate *longitude* (east-west position), because the earth is turning all the time from west to east, and observing the stars is no good unless you know what the time is at the place where you have come from, so that you can compare it with the time at the place where you are, and work out how far round the world you have gone. And nobody had yet invented a clock that would keep time in a ship at sea that was rolling about. An explorer who wanted to find out where he was had to do it by guessing how far he

Two instruments used on ships in the sixteenth century. The astrolabe (left) was to measure the angle of the sun. The sandglass (right) measured time

had travelled, and most guesses were very inaccurate.

VESPUCCI'S SOLUTION

Vespucci worked out a way of calculating longitude. First of all you had to find an anchorage where you could see both eastern and western horizons. Then you used your hourglass to measure the time from sunset to sunrise. You did this several nights running to see how much longer or shorter the nights were getting. Then you could work out when midnight

was, and measure any other time you wanted. Only then did you start looking at the stars. What you wanted next was to time a *conjunction*: the moment when a particular star or planet was passed in the sky by another planet or by the moon. The final stage was to look up in your *almanac* or table of astronomical information to find out when that same conjunction was due to happen in your home port. Then at last you could work out where you were, because the difference in the two times for the same conjunction would give you your distance from home at the rate of

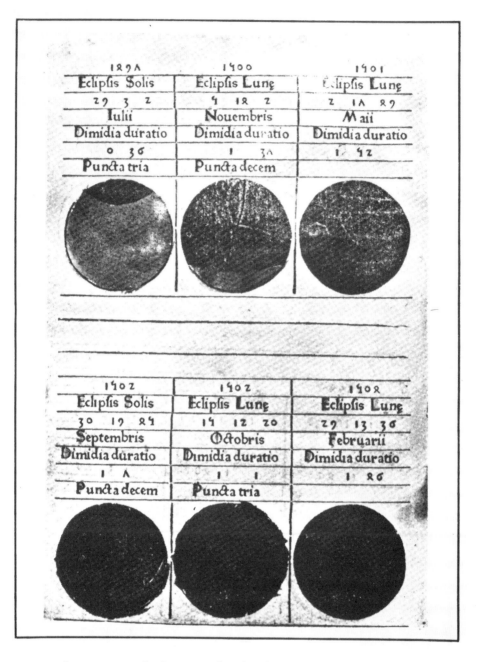

A page from a Spanish almanac of Columbus' time. It shows details of eclipses of the sun and moon

fifteen degrees for every hour. It was a long and clumsy process, but it worked, and it is perhaps the reason why Vespucci deserved to give his name to America rather than Columbus: for Vespucci knew what he had discovered.

Vespucci studies the stars while his crew sleep

THE SIZE OF THE EARTH

When he got home to Spain, Vespucci checked and corrected all his calculations, and revised his estimate of the size of a degree. He now worked out that a degree at the equator was 111 kilometres, and that the circumference of the earth was 39,991 kilometres. He was only eighty kilometres out. After a second voyage in 1501, when he failed to find the Strait of Cattigara, Vespucci decided that Asia was much further west and South America a completely new continent. (D10)

THE CONSEQUENCES

Various people have claimed the credit for discovering America (D11, 12, 13, 14), but, in the end, as Las Casas said of Columbus, 'It was he that put the thread into the hands of the rest'. It was a thread that led European settlers

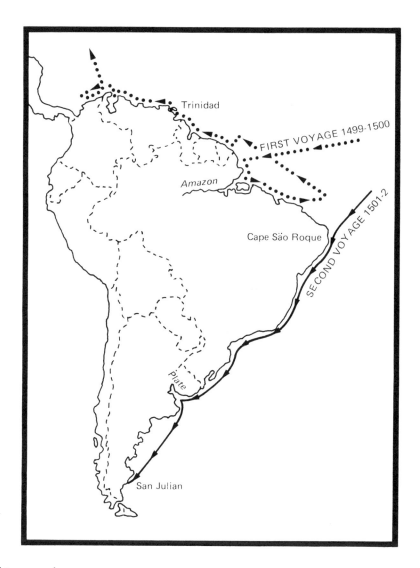

This map shows Vespucci's two voyages. He discovered more miles of the new coastline than any other European explorer

to the mainland, where they conquered and destroyed the great civilizations of Central and South America. (*Ancient America*)

THE CONQUISTADORES

This conquest, begun by Columbus, was continued and extended by other adventurers

known as *conquistadores* (conquerors). (D15) The conquistadores were often minor Spanish nobles who saw in America a chance to make a name for themselves, and to gain land, power and wealth far beyond anything they could hope to get in Spain. (D16) The two most famous conquistadores were Hernan Cortes, and

Francisco Pizarro. Cortes, with a handful of men and a few horses (which terrified the Indians, who had never seen them before), conquered the great Aztec Empire of Mexico in 1519-20. He was able to do so without much difficulty partly because he had guns, and the Indians did not; partly because he was helped by some Indians who resented being ruled by Mexico and paying taxes to the emperor Montezuma (D17); partly because the Indians believed that he was the god who, according to one of their legends, would one day come from the east to rule them. Pizarro, with a similarly small group of men, was successful in much the same way in subduing the Inca Empire of Peru.

THE EMPIRES

Both Cortes and Pizarro, together with their followers, took over the land and people they had conquered in the name of the King of Spain. Others followed them, the area of Spanish control was rapidly extended, and a whole new branch of the Spanish Government was set up to govern the American Empire. Colonies were built on the Spanish model, laws were made to try to ensure that the conquistadores behaved themselves and paid their taxes; officials from Spain checked the way the new colonies were being governed, and made sure the accounts were correct.

Many of the laws made for the colonies show that the Spanish Government was concerned that the Indians should be well treated (D18) and converted to the Catholic faith. (D19) In fact, it was impossible for Spain to prevent the conquistadores from exploiting and ill-treating the Indians (D20),

This German woodcut of 1505 is the earliest known picture of American Indians. Note the cannibal feast on the left. Europeans were very ready to believe that the Indians ate each other

and the native peoples were quickly either enslaved or killed. In Hispaniola alone, the original Indian population, estimated at 250,000, was reduced to about 60,000 by as early as 1508. Ill-treatment and exploitation were not the only killers; many died from European diseases, especially smallpox and measles.

The new lands were organized entirely for the benefit of the European countries: run by European governors, exporting their minerals and crops to Europe. (D21) Potatoes, tomatoes, cocoa, maize and rubber are all crops which came originally from America.

A WIDER WORLD

The discovery of America had important effects on world trade. Europe had paid for imported Asian luxuries by exporting gold and silver. Now she had found a new source of precious metal, and the wealth of America went to pay India and China (as well as the expenses of Spain's European wars). The import of gold and silver also helped to push up prices in Europe, although the main cause of that inflation was the growth of population.

It was no longer possible for Europeans to live in the small, closed world of the Middle Ages. Decisions made by kings and merchants in Europe affected the lives of both Europeans and native people in Africa, America and Asia; and developments in those continents in turn had effects on people in Europe: both on their way of life and on their way of thinking. After Columbus, the world could never be the same again.

DOCUMENT 1

THE RICHES OF CHINA   *MARCO POLO — Describing the extensive luxury trade of Peking, on a journey to China in 1271*

You may take it for a fact that more precious and costly wares are imported into Khan-balik than into any other city in the world. Let me give you particulars. All the treasures that come from India — precious stones, pearls, and other rarities — are brought here. So too are the choicest and costliest products of Cathay itself and every other province. This is on account of the Great Khan himself, who lives here, and of the lords and ladies and the enormous multitude of hotel-keepers and other residents and of visitors who attend the courts held here by the Khan. That is why the volume and value of the imports and of the internal trade exceed those of any other city in the world. It is a fact that every day more than 1,000 cartloads of silk enter the city; for much cloth of gold and silk is woven here. Furthermore, Khan-balik is surrounded by more than 200 other cities, near and far, from which traders come to it to sell and to buy. So it is not surprising that it is the centre of such a traffic as I have described.

DOCUMENT 2

JAPAN   *MARCO POLO – From his own account*

Japan is an island far out at sea to the eastward, some 1,500 miles from the mainland. It is a very big island. The people are fair-complexioned, good-looking, and well-mannered. They are idolaters, wholly independent and exercising no authority over any nation but themselves.

They have gold in great abundance, because it is found there in measureless quantities. And I assure you that no one exports it from the mainland. That is how they come to possess so much of it – so much indeed that I can report to you in sober truth a veritable marvel concerning a certain palace of the ruler of the island. He has a very large palace entirely roofed with fine gold. And the value of it is almost beyond computation. Moreover all the chambers, of which there are many, are likewise paved with fine gold to a depth of more than two fingers' breadth. And the halls and the windows and every other part of the palace are likewise adorned with gold. The palace is of such incalculable richness that any attempt to estimate its value would pass the bounds of the marvellous. They have pearls in abundance, red in colour, very beautiful, large and round. They are worth as much as the white ones, and indeed more. They also have many other precious stones in abundance. It is a very rich island, so that no one could count its riches.

DOCUMENT 3

THE WAY TO CHINA   *MARCO POLO – Writing about a strait leading out of the China Sea towards Sumatra and the Indian Ocean*

On leaving Lokak [Malaya] and sailing southwards for 500 miles, the traveller reaches the island of Bintan [near Singapore] which is a very savage place. The forests are all of sweet-smelling wood of great utility. From here the route runs for sixty miles through a strait between two islands. In many places the water is not more than four paces deep, so that big ships passing through must raise their steering oar, for they have a draught of about four paces.

DOCUMENT 4

AN ESTIMATE   *COLUMBUS – Measuring the length of a degree*

Experience has shown it, I have discussed it with quotations from the Holy Scriptures, and computed it with the situation of the terrestrial paradise which Holy Church has approved. I see that the world is not so large as the common crowd say it is, and that one degree of the Equator is fifty-two miles. This is a fact one can touch with one's fingers. I am not one of those carried astray by the new calculations. The length of a degree is fifty-two miles. This is a fact, and whatever any one says to the contrary is only words.

DOCUMENT 5

COLUMBUS AND SPAIN   *The first agreement between Ferdinand and Isabela, King and Queen of Castile, and Columbus, 17th April 1492. The agreement was drawn up by a secretary, and addressed to the King and Queen*

The things . . . your Highnesses give and declare to Christopher Columbus in some satisfaction for what he has discovered in the oceans, and for the voyage which now, with the aid of God, he is about to make therein, in the service of your Highnesses, are as follows:

Firstly, that your Highnesses make from this time the said Don Christopher Columbus your Admiral in all those islands and mainlands which by his hand and industry shall be discovered or acquired in the said oceans. . . .

Likewise, that your Highnesses make the said Don Christopher your Viceroy and Governor General in all the said islands and mainlands which as has been said, he may discover or acquire in the said seas.

Whatever merchandise, whether it be pearls, precious stones, gold, silver, spices, which may be bought, bartered, discovered, acquired, or obtained within the limits of the said Admiralty, your Highnesses grant henceforth to the said Don Christopher, and will that he may have and take for himself, the tenth part of all of them.

In all the vessels which may be equipped for the said traffic, the said Admiral Don Christopher Columbus may, if he wishes, contribute and pay the eighth part of all that may be expended in the equipment. And he may take of the profit, the eighth part of all which may result from such equipment.

These are executed and despatched in the town of Santa Fe de la Vega de Granada, on the seventeenth day of April in the year of the nativity of our Saviour Jesus Christ one thousand four hundred and ninety-two.

I, THE KING   I, THE QUEEN
By order of the King and of the Queen. John de Coloma

DOCUMENT 6

REACHING AMERICA   *COLUMBUS – Describing, in a letter, the results of his first voyage (15th February 1493)*

Since I know that you will be pleased at the great success with which the Lord has crowned my voyage, I write to inform you how in thirty-three days I crossed from the Canary Islands to the Indies, with the fleet which our most illustrious sovereigns gave me. I found very many islands with large populations and took possession of them all for their Highnesses; this I did by proclamation and unfurled the royal standard. No opposition was offered. . . .

When I reached Cuba, I followed its north coast westwards, and found it so extensive that I thought this must be the mainland, the province of Cathay. I continued on my course, thinking that I should undoubtedly come to some great towns or cities. . . .

I saw another island eighteen leagues eastwards which I then named 'Hispaniola'. . . .

Hispaniola is a wonder. The mountains and hills, the plains and meadow lands are both fertile and beautiful. They are most suitable for planting crops and for raising cattle of all kinds, and there are good sites for building towns and villages. In Hispaniola there are many spices and large mines of gold and other metals. . . .

These islands are richer than I yet know or can say and I have taken possession of them in their Majesties' name. I have taken possession of a large town which is most conveniently situated for the goldfields and for communications with the mainland both here, and there in the territories of the Grand Khan, with which there will be very profitable trade.

DOCUMENT 7

THE TREATY OF TORDESILLAS   *Extract from the Treaty (1494) dividing all newly discovered lands between Spain and Portugal*

It was declared by the representatives of the King and Queen of Castile and of the King of Portugal:

1. That, whereas a certain controversy exists between the said lords as to what lands, of all those discovered in the ocean sea up to the present day, the date of this treaty, pertain to each one of the said parts respectively; therefore, for the sake of peace and concord, and for the preservation of the relationship and love of the said King of Portugal for the said King and Queen of Castile, they agreed that a boundary or straight line be determined and drawn north and south, on the said ocean sea, from the Arctic to the Antarctic pole. This boundary or line shall be drawn straight, as aforesaid, at a distance of three hundred and seventy leagues west of the Cape Verde Islands. And all lands, found and discovered already, or to be found and discovered hereafter, by the said King of Portugal and by his vessels on this side of the said line towards the east, shall belong to, and remain in the possession of, the said King of Portugal and his successors. And all other lands, which have been discovered or shall be discovered by the said King and Queen of Castile and by their

vessels, on the western side of the said bound, shall belong to the said King and Queen of Castile, and to their successors. . . .

Given in the town of Arevalo, on the second day of the month of July, in the year of the nativity of our Lord Jesus Christ, 1494.

I, THE KING   I, THE QUEEN   I, THE PRINCE

DOCUMENT 8

COLUMBUS'S COMPLAINTS   *COLUMBUS – Complaining of his disgrace and ill-treatment in a letter to King Ferdinand and Queen Isabela, 7th July 1503*

I spent seven years at your royal court, where everyone to whom I spoke of this undertaking said that it was ridiculous. Now even tailors are asking for licences of exploration. The lands that here obey your Highnesses are greater and richer than all the rest of Christendom. I had, by God's will, placed them under your royal and exalted rule, and was on the point of securing very great revenues. I was happy and I was secure. Then, when I was waiting for ships to carry me into your royal presence, a victor bearing great news of gold, I and my two brothers were suddenly arrested and put aboard a ship, naked, ill-treated and loaded with chains; and this without trial or sentence.

I came to serve at the age of twenty-eight and today I have not a hair on my head that is not grey. My body is sick and wasted. All that I and my brothers had has been taken from us, down to our very coats, without my being heard or seen, and I have suffered great dishonour.

The restoration of my honour and of what has been taken from me and the punishment of the man who inflicted this damage on me will redound to your Highnesses' good name. It would be a most virtuous deed and a famous example if you were to do this, and would leave to Spain a glorious memory of your Highnesses as grateful and just princes.

DOCUMENT 9

A NEW CONTINENT?   *COLUMBUS – Still insisting, in a letter to the King and Queen during his fourth voyage (7th July 1503), that the lands which he had discovered are in Asia*

In all these places I had visited, I had found the information given me were true, and this assured me that the same would be so of the province of Ciguare [the area containing the Maya city of Guatemala], which, as they told me, lies inland nine days' journey westward. . . . They say also that Ciguare is surrounded by water, and that ten days' journey away is the river Ganges. . . .

I arrived on 13th May at the province of Mago [Macaca in Cuba], which borders on Cathay.

It is said that inland in the country lying towards Cathay they have gold-embroidered materials.

DOCUMENT 10

A NEW CONTINENT   *AMERIGO VESPUCCI — Announcing his discovery of a new continent in a letter to Lorenzo de Medici (1502)*

We departed from the above-mentioned Cape Verde very easily, having taken in everything necessary, such as water and wood and other requirements essential for putting to sea across the ocean wastes in search of new land. We sailed on the wind within half a point of southwest, so that in sixty-four days we arrived at a new land which, for many reasons that are enumerated in what follows, we observed to be a continent.

We found the land thickly inhabited. I noted there the wonders of God and of nature, of which I determined to inform your Excellency, as I have done of my other voyages.

DOCUMENT 11

THE VIKING DISCOVERY OF AMERICA   *An inscription from the Vinland Map*

By God's will, after a long voyage from the island of Greenland to the south toward the most distant remaining parts of the western ocean sea, sailing southward amidst the ice, the companions Bjarni and Leif Eiriksson discovered a new land, extremely fertile and even having vines, the which island they named Vinland. Eric legate of the Apostolic See [that is, representative of the Pope] and bishop of Greenland and the neighbouring regions, arrived in this truly vast and very rich land, in the name of Almighty God, in the last year of our most blessed father Pascal [the Pope], remained a long time in both summer and winter, and later returned northeastward toward Greenland and then proceeded [i.e. home to Europe] in most humble obedience to the will of his superiors.

DOCUMENT 12

AN ENGLISH VOYAGE TO NORTH AMERICA   *JOHN DAY — Writing to Columbus with information about previous voyages to North America (probably written in 1497 or 1498)*

Your Lordship will see that the cape closest to Ireland is 1,800 miles west of Dursey Head, [in County Cork, south-west Ireland] which is in Ireland. . . .

It is considered certain that this same point of land at another time was found and discovered by the men of Bristol. [Nobody knows when this was. It might have been within the previous year or two, after Columbus's first voyage, or it might have been before Columbus first sailed to the West Indies.]

DOCUMENT 13

SOUTH AMERICA   *COLUMBUS – In his journal for 15th August 1498 he realizes that South America is a new continent*

I believe that this is a very great continent, until today unknown. And reason aids me greatly because of that so great river and fresh-water sea, and next, the saying of Esdras. . . that the six parts of the world are of dry land, and one of water. . . . Which book of Esdras St Ambrose approved in his *Exameron* and so St Augustine in the passage *morietur filius meus Christus* as Francisco de Mayrones alleges; and further I am supported by the saying of many Carib Indians whom I took at other times, who said that to the south of them was mainland . . . and they said that in it there was much gold. . . . And if this be a continent, it is a marvellous thing, and will be so among all the wise, since so great a river flows that it makes a fresh-water sea of 48 leagues.

DOCUMENT 14

COLUMBUS AND AMERICA   *BARTOLOME DE LAS CASAS – A Spanish priest who went to Hispaniola just after Columbus supporting Columbus's claim to have discovered America*

Others, besides Pinzon and De Solis [two later Spanish explorers], say it is all one coast from Paria [on the mainland of South America], though provinces have different names and there are also different languages. This, then, was declared by witnesses who had been there and knew it well by having used their own eyes, and now it would be needless to seek for further witnesses than in the grocers' shops in Seville. Thus it cannot be denied to the Admiral [i.e. Columbus], except with great injustice, that as he was the first discoverer of those Indies, so he was also of the whole of our mainland, and to him is due the credit, by discovering the province of Paria, which is a part of all that land. For it was he that put the thread into the hands of the rest, by which they found the clew (sic) to more distant parts.

DOCUMENT 15

EXPLORING THE WEST INDIES   *BERNAL DIAZ – Born in 1492,*
he went with Cortes to conquer Mexico. In his old age he wrote
History of the Conquest of New Spain

My father and one of my brothers being in the service of the Catholic
Kings, Don Ferdinand and Dona Isabela, I wished in some sort to emulate
them. When, therefore, in the year 1514 a gentleman named Pedrarias
Davila went out as Governor of Tierra Firme (on the coast of Panama), I
agreed to accompany him to the newly conquered country.... As news
had reached us that the island of Cuba had lately been conquered and
settled, under the governorship of a kinsman of mine, some of us gentle-
men and persons of quality decided to ask permission to go there.

Once we had received permission we boarded a good ship, and with
fair weather reached the island of Cuba. On landing we paid our respects
to the Governor, who was pleased to see us and promised to give us
Indians as soon as there were any to spare. I was at that time twenty-
four.

After spending three fruitless years in Tierra Firme and Cuba, about a
hundred and ten of us, settlers from Tierra Firme or Spaniards who had
come to Cuba but received no grant of Indians, decided to make an
expedition to seek new lands in which to try our fortunes and find
occupation.

We found ourselves in possession of three ships loaded with cassava
bread, which is made from a root, and we bought pigs, which cost us
three pesos each. At that time there were no sheep or cattle in the island
of Cuba, for it was only beginning to be settled. We added a supply of oil
and some inexpensive articles for barter. We then sought out three
pilots.... We also engaged the necessary sailors, and the best supply we
could get of ropes, cordage, cables, and anchors, of casks for water, and
everything else we needed for our voyage.

DOCUMENT 16

LOOKING FOR RICHES   *BERNAL DIAZ – From his account of*
the conquest of Mexico

Many interested readers have asked me why the true Conquistadors who
won New Spain, and the great and strong city of Mexico did not stay to
settle, but went on to other provinces. I think this question is justified,
and I will give them an answer. Learning from Montezuma's account-
books the names of the places which sent him tributes of gold, and where
the mines and chocolate and cotton-cloths were to be found, we decided
to go to these places; and our resolve was strengthened... when we
realized that there were no gold or mines or cotton in the towns around

Mexico, only a lot of maize and the *maguey* plantations from which they obtained their wine. For this reason we thought of it as a poor land, and went off to colonize other provinces. But we were thoroughly deceived.

DOCUMENT 17

THE CONQUEST OF MEXICO *HERNAN CORTES – Who con-quered the Aztecs of Mexico in 1519, makes an alliance with the Indians of Cempoala against Mexico*

The chiefs of Cempoala asked Cortes what was to be done, for all the forces of Mexico and of the great Montezuma would descend upon them, and they could not possibly escape death and destruction.

Cortes replied with a most cheerful smile that he and his brothers who were with him would defend them and kill anyone who tried to harm them; and the chiefs and their villagers one and all promised to stand by us, to obey any orders we might give them, and to join their forces with ours against Montezuma and his allies. . . .

As they now paid no more tribute and the tax-gatherers had dis-appeared, they could not contain their delight at having thrown off the tyranny of the Mexicans.

DOCUMENT 18

THE TREATMENT OF INDIANS *Extracts from the Laws of Burgos, issued in Spain, 27th December 1512*

XV
Since the most important consideration for the good treatment and increase of the Indians is their subsistence, we order and command that all persons who have Indians shall be obliged to maintain those who are on their estates, and there to keep continual sufficiency of bread and yams and peppers.

XXIV
We command that no person or persons shall dare to beat any Indian with sticks, or whip him, or call him dog, or address him by any name other than his proper name alone.

DOCUMENT 19

CHRISTIANITY *Extract from the Laws of Burgos*

IV
We command that every two weeks the person who has (the Indians) in charge shall examine them to see what each one knows particularly and

to teach them the Ten Commandments and the Seven Deadly Sins and the Articles of the Faith.

DOCUMENT 20

SPANISH CRUELTY   *LAS CASAS — Describing the ill-treatment of* *the Indians (1542)*

The Spaniards came with their horsemen well armed with swords and lances, making a cruel havoc and slaughter among them, overrunning cities and towns, and sparing neither sex nor age. Nor did their cruelty take pity on women with children, whose bellies they ripped up, taking out the infants to hew them to pieces. They would often lay wagers as to who could cut a man through the middle with most dexterity, or who could cut off his head with one blow. The children they would take by the feet and dash their innocent heads against rocks, and when they were fallen in the water, the Spaniards would call upon them to swim with a strange and cruel derision. Sometimes they would run both the mother and unborn infant through in one thrust.

DOCUMENT 21

USING THE NEW LANDS   *HERNAN CORTES — In a letter to the* *Spanish King*

I assure your . . . Majesty that, could we but obtain plants and seeds from Spain, and if Your Highness would be pleased to order them sent to us . . . the ability of these natives in cultivating the soil and making plantations would very shortly produce such abundance that great profit would accrue to the Imperial Crown of your Highness. . . .

ACKNOWLEDGMENTS

Illustrations

Mansell Collection pages 2, 11, 12, 13, 16, 19; the National Maritime Museum page 17

Documents

D1, 2, 3, *The Travels of Marco Polo,* ed. and tr. R.E. Latham, Penguin Classics 1958; D4, 10, 14, *Amerigo Vespucci Pilot Major,* F.J. Pohl, Frank Cass & Co. Ltd; D6, 8, 9, 16, 17, *The Four Voyages of Christopher Columbus,* ed. and tr. J.M. Cohen, Penguin Classics 1969; D13, *Christopher Columbus Master Mariner,* S.E. Morison, New English Library; D16, 17, *The Conquest of New Spain,* ed. and tr. J.M. Cohen, Penguin Classics 1963; D18, 19, 20, *The Spanish Tradition in America,* C. Gibson, Harper & Row Ltd.

Greenhaven World History Program

History Makers
Alexander
Constantine
Leonardo Da Vinci
Columbus
Luther, Erasmus and Loyola
Napoleon
Bolivar
Adam Smith, Malthus and Marx
Darwin
Bismark
Henry Ford
Roosevelt
Stalin
Mao Tse-Tung
Gandhi
Nyerere and Nkrumah

Great Civilizations
The Ancient Near East
Ancient Greece
Pax Romana
The Middle Ages
Spices and Civilization
Chingis Khan and the Mongol Empire
Akbar and the Mughal Empire
Traditional China
Ancient America
Traditional Africa
Asoka and Indian Civilization
Mohammad and the Arab Empire
Ibin Sina and the Muslim World
Suleyman and the Ottoman Empire

Great Revolutions
The Neolithic Revolution
The Agricultural Revolution
The Scientific Revolution
The Industrial Revolution
The Communications Revolution
The American Revolution
The French Revolution
The Mexican Revolution
The Russian Revolution
The Chinese Revolution

Enduring Issues
Cities
Population
Health and Wealth
A World Economy
Law
Religion
Language
Education
The Family

Political and Social Movements
The Slave Trade
The Enlightenment
Imperialism
Nationalism
The British Raj and Indian Nationalism
The Growth of the State
The Suez Canal
The American Frontier
Japan's Modernization
Hitler's Reich
The Two World Wars
The Atom Bomb
The Cold War
The Wealth of Japan
Hollywood